FREMANTLE POETS

TWO POETS

Andrew Lansdown · Kevin Gillam

Introduction by Lisa Gorton

First published 2011 by FREMANTLE PRESS
25 Quarry Street, Fremantle 6160
(PO Box 158, North Fremantle 6159)
Western Australia
www.fremantlepress.com.au

Consultant editor Georgia Richter
Cover designer Allyson Crimp
Cover image James Wills
Printed by Everbest Printing Company, China

National Library of Australia Cataloguing-in-Publication entry

Gillam, Kevin.
Two Poets / Kevin Gillam; Andrew Lansdown
1st ed.
ISBN 9781921696602 (pbk)
ISBN 9781921696619 (electronic resource)

Fremantle poets; 2
Other authors/contributors:
Lansdown, Andrew, 1954–

A821.4

 The Publisher gratefully acknowledges
the City of Fremantle for assistance with
publication of this title.

FREMANTLE POETS

TWO POETS

Andrew Lansdown · Kevin Gillam

Introduction by Lisa Gorton

FREMANTLE
fine independent publishing PRESS

CONTENTS

LISA GORTON lives in Melbourne. Her first poetry collection, *Press Release*, was shortlisted for the Mary Gilmore Poetry Prize and the Melbourne Prize Best Writing Award, and won the 2008 Victorian Premier's Prize for Poetry. Lisa has also been awarded the Vincent Buckley Poetry Prize. She wrote a doctorate on John Donne's poetry and prose, and has written a children's novel, *Cloudland*.

INTRODUCTION

Lisa Gorton

Here are two markedly different Western Australian poets. Both pay attention to small facts of nature. Both treat poetry as a work of intimacy, not performance. In tone, both poets are closer to the voice of the diary than of the café or pub. Even when they deal, as they often do, with suburban domestic life, their poems mark out a place of inwardness. Yet their collections reflect and create different imaginative worlds. In particular, these two poets relate differently to time: Lansdown's poems work to distil and preserve a single moment, whereas Gillam's work to capture the moment-by-moment experience of time. Intriguingly, their writing habits reflect this difference. Lansdown works in a study, seated at a window, looking out. Gillam gets ideas for poems walking the back lanes around where he lives. This difference could be said to define the nature of each poet's achievement.

Lansdown engages consistently, though by no means exclusively, with the austere Japanese tradition. Almost all his collections include haiku or tanka sequences: short poems in syllabic verse that capture a single observation in exact and simple words. As one of Lansdown's poems puts it, 'Haiku are pebbles/ poets lob into the pond/ of our emotions'. Landown brings that understated discipline to his descriptions of the Australian landscape.

The Australian painter Fred Williams once remarked that Australia's landscape has no vanishing point. Working with haiku, Lansdown frees his poems from what you might call the argument of foreground and background. His are small-scale, exact observations. As a consequence, his haiku and short poems about birds and flowers achieve a sense of place remarkably free of the usual rhetoric of landscape. They are one of the best reasons to read this collection.

Over nearly forty years, Lansdown has worked at this art of precision. Most of the poems collected here are new, but there are some from his award-winning 1993 collection, *Between Glances*, and some from his 2004 collection, *Fontanelle*. He started some of the poems newly published here more than a decade ago. Nonetheless, this selection has the coherence you might expect of a single collection. Together, these poems show how an aesthetic of exact detail and subtle craft has shaped his poetic idiom – has become the very language of his thought.

Even many of the longer poems work with the kind of precision that haiku requires. Take 'Fontanelle', for instance – one of the standout poems in this collection. A poem of seven two-line stanzas, it maintains the lucidity and efficiency of haiku. It starts, 'Strange, this seeing/ the heart in the head'. In this poem, the first line of each stanza has four syllables, the second, five: a heart-beat rhythm worked not by word-stress patterns, but by line lengths. But Lansdown is typically understated, and combines this clean use of language with a tone of unforced directness.

If you were to express in architecture the various styles of poetry, the place where Lansdown writes could serve as an image of haiku. This dedicated room, with a desk at the window, suggests at once haiku's containment and its commitment to looking out. It is characteristic of Lansdown's straightforwardness that a number of poems in this collection make reference to this writing room. He writes in 'This Abundance' of 'Stepping out of my study'. 'Disturbance' starts, 'Again from the corner/ of my writing-room window ...'. But perhaps the most memorable of these writing-room poems is 'The Visitor':

My landlord's small, blond-haired boy
comes daily to peer through my windows –
four oblongs of glass forming the corner
of the room against which my writing desk
is nestled. My sunpanels and pleasures.

Lansdown has written three children's novels and this poem illustrates with what ease he can work with narrative. In this case, the boy's interruption pushes the poem past its single moment: Lansdown imagines the boy's view from outside, looking in. This outside view prompts a meditation on the nature of his work: 'I have come to this room/ wanting not visitors, but visitations.'

There is almost always in Lansdown's work this sense of the window: clear, polished, made for looking out. Though the celebration of nature might be said to be the defining motive of his work, it is nature in itself he seeks to celebrate – not for him the Romantic tradition of finding the mind in the world. As a consequence, his poems, for all their play of sound, have a quality of stillness: the space of the page around them seems charged with silence. His poems typically capture not the experience of life in time, but the experience of moments outside time – visitations. For this reason, his poems often work with cameras, windows and reflections. His poem 'Macro Movements' illustrates his poetic ambition to still the single moment in its fleetingness: 'On macro setting –/ I'm trying to photograph/ a bee on the buzz … As my camera/ clicks, it flits to my finger –/ the red dragonfly.' Perhaps his tanka 'Signal' is so intriguing because the setting serves as an image of how the poem itself works – with a sense of distance, closed in its small frame:

As I lift the mug,
light reflects from its glazing
in the black window –
faint and intermittent like
a lighthouse signal, far off.

Kevin Gillam has also taken up haiku. Indeed, his poem 'untitled' is one of the most satisfying in this collection: 'pissing in the lane,/ staining the pickets, unthreading/ the rope of ants'. Yet at once, in this small poem, you glimpse the difference between these two poets: Gillam's poems set him in the midst of time, in the present participle, and in the frame. 'If, then, time present ... comes into existence only because it passes into time past, how can we say that even this *is*, since the cause of its being is that it will pass away ...': Augustine's brilliant investigation of time in *The Confessions* defines the conditions of Gillam's poetic style: its restlessness, its desire to break open boundaries and test how consciousness might find some holding structure.

Gillam's is a various and wide-ranging art – the art of the solitary walker. His poem 'passacaglia' starts, 'me I'm out scouring back lanes for/ moments of leaving – raven's feather, at/ certain angles indigo, rubbing/ palms across fretting brickwork ...'. This poem, which describes his writing process, serves also as his manifesto. It illustrates how his poems attend not to the still moment, but to the haphazard and open-ended experience of time: 'pulling me through tenses, was to is'.

As this poem 'passacaglia' suggests, Gillam gets ideas for poems walking the back laneways where he lives. Places withdrawn, intimate, and full of sudden glimpses, their character defines the character of these poems, which have a walker's unaffiliated attentiveness to small facts.

Not for Gillam the cartwheel and *arms up!* fiat of the professional gymnast. His poems sidestep the whole idea of performance. They seek not to still experience in art, but to enact it. For this reason, his line breaks work against any sense of an ending. He breaks phrases, and sometimes words: 'out here, a different/ quality of silence, as if/ sifted, as if wrung of // possibility, as/ if notes, the missing fourth and sev-/ enth from a pentaton-// ic scale ...' ('out here'). In this way, he works against closure. His lines, always drawing the eye down the page, capture instead the digressive freedom of someone walking.

Gillam's life as a musician brings another element to his experience of landscape. A professional cellist and music teacher, Gillam grew up immersed in music. Every Saturday night, his family listened to records. In this collection, several poems – including 'chromos' and 'songs sul G' – deal directly with his life in music. But music is all through this collection; it has entered the landscape. His wonderful poem 'Blackwood' holds a place between sight and sound:

> the congregation of tuarts
> stands shabby while your surface
> has gone to pewter and the diff-
>
> erence is ocean has barlines of
> waves and the measure of tide while
> you are one endless bar played
> at gravity's tempo and a chitta-
> chitta flits electric ...

Here, landscape and music work as images of each other. That layering gives this poem its particular intimacy. If visual images place things in space, sounds have a floating quality. As a consequence, here the landscape works at once as a place and as a fact of consciousness.

'Blackwood', 'Carnaby's', 'Con's, 1968', '(for the siblings)', 'gliss', 'the colour of disruption', 'the furniture of thought', 'the unwritten blue': these poems work with longer lines and interwoven images, because they recreate not the fragmentary present but the more complete landscape of memory. 'the unwritten blue' starts with the word 'remember'. In these poems, Gillam takes up the Romantic tradition that has shaped so much Australian writing. They mark a new and exciting development in Gillam's work – together they make, perhaps, the first part of his suburban Australian Prelude.

Here are two Western Australian poets with a remarkable sense of place; two poets who, together, show how that sense of place depends on their idea of poetry, and its life in time.

THE COLOUR OF LIFE

Andrew Lansdown

ANDREW LANSDOWN's poetry publications include *Homecoming* (Fremantle Arts Centre Press, 1979), *Counterpoise* (Angus & Robertson, 1982), *Windfalls* (FACP, 1984), *Waking and Always* (A&R, 1987; Picaro Press, 2007), *The Grasshopper Heart* (Collins/A&R, 1991), *Between Glances* (William Heinemann Australia, 1993), *Fontanelle* (Five Islands Press, 2004), *Birds in Mind: Australian Nature Poems* (Wombat Books, 2009) and *Far From Home: Poems of Faith, Grief and Gladness* (Wombat Books, 2010). Andrew has won many poetry awards, including the Western Australian Premier's Award (twice) and the Adelaide Festival's John Bray National Poetry Award. Andrew is also a widely published children's poet and novelist. For more information on Andrew's work, visit: http://andrewlansdown.com.

ACKNOWLEDGEMENTS

Many poems in this collection (some in slightly altered form) have been previously published in the following magazines, newspapers and anthologies: *The Alternative, Antipodes* (USA), *The Best Australian Poems 2006, The Best Australian Poems 2008, Between Glances, Birds in Mind, Blue Dog, The Bulletin, The Canberra Times, Courier Mail, Fontanelle, Island, Lynx* (USA), *Northern Perspective, Quadrant, Southern Review, Studio, Verse* (Scotland), *The Weekend Australian, The West Australian* and *Westerly.*

The poet acknowledges with gratitude that some poems in this collection were written with the financial assistance of the Literature Board of the Australia Council for the Arts.

CONTENTS

Finishing Up

Nightfall … and I am still here
in the school at the prison farm.

My children will be at the table, filling
their mouths with food and chatter.

And the littlest one will be asking
her mother, 'Where is Daddy?'

I am where my resignation
has led me. My roguish students

are in the compound, locked up
for the night. Except for the sentries

the guards are gone. I am alone,
finishing up. Did I miss someone

when I said goodbye? Does it matter?
We have been good to one another,

these bad men and I. I try not
to think I will never see them again.

I am alone. I look out the window.
The forest is in silhouette.

On the lawn, almost dissolved
in the dusk, a young kangaroo

hunches on its haunches to graze.
It was not there a moment ago and

in a moment when I open the door
it will not be there again.

Wattles by Water

i

Fishing for redfin
with green rods, wattles scatter
pollard on a pool.

ii

The wattle blossom
on the slow current – comets
with tails of pollen.

iii

Riverbank wattles –
spattering the brown water ·
with their yellow spawn.

The Nemesia

Cast in the green
of the bud
a bell
of beaten gold

The nemesia
the first to knell
the winter
has one … then
four flowers

A carillon
chiming pale yellows
to the gusty air's
glancing blows

The Colour of Life

Why is it that here in this café,
a hard wind harmless on the window,
a bright fire coughing in the grate,
scones and tea on the table, I feel

suddenly, strangely sad? Why is it,
and what? A loneliness, a longing –
not, it seems, in spite of, but
because of, the loveliest of things.

It is the colour of life. *Sabi*
the haiku poets would say. I say
too much. I break a scone and steam
wafts from the wound, like

the spirit of a just man, going home.

Gradations of Black

i

In my lower back
pain defines the many de-
gradations of black.

ii

It is so mundane
this misery masterminded
by persistent pain.

iii

I try to recall
gladness ... but in pain's presence
endurance is all.

iv

Morning until late
pain impresses on my spine
sensations of hate.

Prayer Against Pain

If you love me still
oh Lord make me well

Let your goodness spill
to this place I fell

Lift me by your will
high above this hell

By your power kill
pain's clangour and knell

Let my body fill
with harm's last farewell

And my being thrill
with cruelty's quell

Oh Lord make me still
if you love me well

Menace

It's not just the colours,
the burnt-out blacks and blazing oranges

It's not just the flying,
the buzzing wings and erratic barging

It's also the walking,
the stop-starting and upstart dart-poking

With all the while the wings
rigid and out-jutting from the thorax ...

Yes, above all, the wings,
those at-the-ready wind-whetted switchblades

Wings angled like the arms
of a bad man, a madman, hands on hips

Elbows crooked defiant,
daring any hothead to take him on –

The spider-hunting wasp
roving on and around the garden rocks

Macro Movements

i

On macro setting –
I'm trying to photograph
a bee on the buzz.

ii

In the photograph
a blurred impression of legs –
the grasshopper leap.

iii

As my camera
clicks, it flits to my finger –
the red dragonfly.

Bird and Bull

The dotterel,
stalking, sniping – so little
by the muzzle
and muddy hoof of the bull
drinking at the dam's puddle.

Cattle in Irrigated Pasture

The cocky and his hand
are squatting by a tractor
looking at a herd of Aberdeens
in an irrigated paddock.

Along the fence, a line
of impact sprinklers fire
and ratchet. Beyond the fence
the paddocks are bare.

The two men are as quiet
as their cattle. Each beast
is bankable, they think,
pleased. They take pleasure, too,

in the inadvertent beauty.
This bonus on their labours!
For a moment they are émigrés
from economics, and simply

enjoy the sight of the sleek
black heifers grazing at random
by the spurting water
in the green hock-high sorghum.

Lilies

Lady, the lilies
we admired in the paddock,
the arum lilies
so whitely lovely, have died
from the farmer's herbicide.

Warrior Monk

i

A warrior monk,
the heron stands at the brink
of the floating world.

ii

Spear at the ready
the heron warrior monk
meditates on death.

iii

Meditation, step
the heron warrior monk
resignation, stab.

iv

The grey heron's koan:
the monk and the warrior,
how can they combine?

Rising Upriver

During the night the sea
closed up the sandbar we

dug open in the day.
Now upriver a way

water's slowly welling –
covering and filling

the prints a heron left
impressed on the mudflat.

Pelican Haiku

i

Identical slant –
the beaks of the buoyant
harbour pelicans.

ii

The calm water –
an incoming pelican
barefoot skiing.

iii

As if moth-eaten –
the pink pouch of a pelican
by the fishing pier.

iv

Racquets ready –
pelicans in the harbour
playing lacrosse.

v

Ring reinforcements –
those yellow circles around
the pelican's eyes.

vi

Beak to eye to neck –
pelican pretending to be
a sprung safety-pin!

vii

A different angle –
one pelican in the flock
has lifted its beak.

Postpartum Elation

After the long pain –
such brightness on her face as
she held our firstborn,
his head still messy with blood
and vernix and forceps-marks!

Fontanelle

Strange, this seeing
the heart in the head.

Look, a drumming
in the cranium,

a tom-tomming
against the membrane

where the bones are
yet to meet and knit.

May they never
knit entirely, son.

May head and heart
beat in unison

always, as now
in your fontanelle.

This Darkness

Something has smothered his smiles,
those wide-gummed, ten-week grins.
Perhaps it is me. Perhaps he knows
I could not return them. What is this
darkness? Never mind, baby. Never
mind me. Calm is a form of gladness.
And you are calm, calm on my knee.
Your stare on my face, your grasp
on my finger. And yet this darkness.
Oh, keep a grip, keep a grip on me!

Misery

A misery has gripped him, gotten him
by the heart, the throat. All morning,
he has been crying, bawling, howling.
What is it? For goodness sakes what!

Oh son, son! Although your unreasoned
unrelenting cries strain my restraints,
badger me to battery, don't think I don't
sympathise. Don't think I haven't felt

that misery, and felt it often. I know
how it gets hold of you, gets hold
even in the good times, and slams you
face-down to the fist-pounding floor.

Black

i

As I did not die
in my sleep, my heart starts up
its pining again.

ii

A beautiful day …
so there's no way to explain
why I feel this way.

iii

After me once more –
black dog! The grip of its jaw,
the scratch of its paw!

iv

So blindingly black …
as when the shining world turns
to the sun its back.

Signal

As I lift the mug,
light reflects from its glazing
in the black window –
faint and intermittent like
a lighthouse signal, far off.

Human

Not ingratitude
but … human … to be feeling
on the quiet beach
towards sunset in autumn
such loneliness and longing.

Me

'In this mortal frame
of mine ... there is something ...' *
Yes, it's me ... and I
feel this *me* always yearning
for something that is not me.

* Matsuo Basho, 'Learn from the Pine'

In a Café

Her voice is very low, like a man's.
This pleasing discrepancy: that deep voice
from those thin lips, that slender neck.

She is speaking to a young man
who has his back to me. He wears
a cravat at his throat, like a dandy.

She smiles at him, gazing
into his eyes then into her cup.
She mostly speaks, he mostly listens.

Perhaps he likes the sound of it,
her mellow voice – the very voice
she uses indiscriminately every day –

the voice that says, 'This cake
is too sweet', or 'My feet hurt', or
'I love you' – the voice she hears

day and night without astonishment.
Unwittingly, she is womanly with him,
winsome, glancing up and down, the curtains

of her long hair (curled tight and
stained dark from the unseasonable rain)
swinging against her high cheek bones.

She glances and smiles and unsmiles
like a Mona Lisa. He mostly listens. And I,
being alone and at the next table,

entirely listen. The words are
indistinct, the melody the only meaning
I understand. The suds of a cappuccino

cling to the rim of my empty cup.
And then she says (not more loudly than
anything else but somehow more clearly),

'His uncle murdered his wife.'
The words splash above the current
of her voice, which runs on in a murmur.

Not the misery but the ambiguity grips me.
I wonder, whose wife did the uncle kill?
His own or his nephew's? And why? And what

does the dandy think of it? He pays
for the coffees and they step into
the wet street, into the shining bitumen

blackness, almost touching each other.

Going Down

As on a treadmill,
a woman on the steps of
the escalator –
beckoning a small boy who
fears to join her going down.

Getting Wet

Driving to the beach, we pass
a cemetery. 'What's that place?'
my youngest daughter asks.

Who is equal to a child's
questions? Who except Jesus
is equal to death's?

I ponder what to say.
'That's where they bury
people when they die.'

In the ocean she clings
to me, unafraid. She imagines
I'm stronger than the surf.

The waves swell. The sky
grows as grey as a headstone
and then begins to sob.

The roads are gutters.
Bleary through the windscreen
the graveyard reappears.

My child is full of care:
'Oh, the poor people! Won't they
get wet under there?'

The Visitor

for Nicholas

My landlord's small, blond-haired boy
comes daily to peer through my windows –
four oblongs of glass forming the corner
of the room against which my writing desk
is nestled. My sunpanels and pleasures.

Disadvantaged by the light, he presses
his pale face to a pane and cups his hands
about his eyes, trying to gaze in at me
without glare. Yes, his eyes confirm,
the man is there, sitting still as always.

Often he startles me, having approached
on his bare feet as quietly as a cat
on its paws. He stares in now, the glass
glazing with his breath. I glance at him
and smile. But only briefly, hoping

neither to encourage nor discourage him.
For after all, I have come to this room
wanting not visitors but visitations.
And he seems perfectly to understand.
He watches quietly for a moment then

leaves. Today, out of sweet courtesy,
he returned, touched the window, and said,
'I'm going now.' I smiled and nodded,
and wondered if I ought to press my palm
to the glass, as I have seen prisoners do

before their loved ones leave the visiting
room and the gaol to go free in the world.

Homecoming

It is thrilling to be so loved.
Hearing my step on the verandah
he bellows to Mum that I'm home
and races to the door to greet me.

To be so loved. It is thrilling.
Seeing me he bursts into welcome,
with glad prattle, great prancing
and that sheer shine on his face!

Altered State

Having heard it once
the mosquito's in no state
to hear it once more:
The answer to the famed koan
concerning one hand clapping.

Naming

The operculum, the cap
that crimps the filaments –

see how this one fallen
from a Tasmanian blue gum

is pimpled and knobbled
like the rosette comb

of a silky bantam rooster.
Indeed, maybe the likeness

should be reversed? Maybe
long ago the conceited birds

took to crowning themselves
with the gumtrees' caps,

until the caps became
flesh in permanent graft?

A cross-Kingdom evolution?
Whatever, I suggest that

as the tree after its cap
so the fowl after its crown

should be named – for truly,
Eucalyptus or *Bantamus*,

both are boldly *Globulus*!

Images of Inflorescence

Eucalyptus caesia

i

Brushed with bloom,
the buds of the gungurru gum
are like newborn babies
coated with vernix caseosa.

ii

Each bud is a jade urn
(see the hairline crack
where the lid lifts?) packed
not with ash but with fire.

iii

Each red flower has
an Afro hair-style –
a yellow bead tied
to the end of every thread.

iv

The flowers are a corps de ballet –
their slim, white waists
and crimson tutus,
the froufrou of their dancing.

Spores

i

Furtively lifting
a fern frond. Oh-oh, which dot
is the microfilm?

ii

Unbelievable –
innumerable ferns in Braille
on the frond's blind side!

iii

On the windowsill
fine red dust ... perhaps, tree fern,
it's outback bulldust?

iv

Dusting the dish
for the culprit's fingerprints –
the wild mushrooms.

Wattle Pod

A little swelling,
lovely in the slenderness
of the wattle pod ...
Feel it, this rubbable bump,
this fabulous tree in braille.

Birds and Figs

Silvereye vandals
in the fig tree's pottery –
randomly striking
the neckless jugs, leaving red
gashes in the green glazing.

For the Finches

i

A garden sprinkler –
luring with its soft whirring
a flock of finches.

ii

The zebra finches –
fluffing and preening beneath
the spinning sprinkler.

iii

Not for the lawn
but for the finches – I turn
the sprinkler on.

This Abundance

The thing that astonishes me is that
life goes on abundantly without me.
Stepping out of my study, I discover
magpies have made a nest not twenty
metres from the house. By the gate

the buds of the *Eucalyptus preissiana*
are a hatching of chickens: a yellow
fuzz beneath the raised opercula.
A small girl skips along the road,
her hair in a pony tail, flouncing.

A neighbour hails me for a yarn.
'Yes,' he says. 'This old bloke lived
in a thousand gallon tank at Kulikup
and cut sleepers with an adze.'
His memory is almost twice my age.

As we talk, his dog paws at a puddle
in the gravel, then pokes its muzzle
into the muddy water – sticks its face
in right up to its ears! Fancy that!
Fancy a dog doing that – and me there

to see it! Truly, it's an astonishment,
this abundance independent of me
that touches me seemingly by accident.

Holiday

My son, standing on the water
behind a boat, buoyant with speed;

my daughter, scooping a jellyfish,
a bluebottle with a whitebait in its bowl;

three cygnets, air in their bones,
swimming in single file in the bay;

a squid in the torchlight,
blushing black before my crab-net:

these things this day at the sea,
this holiday, holy day, full of wonders.

Eskimo-Kiss

i

Is it you, violet,
who taught the Arctic lovers
to Eskimo-kiss?

ii

Breathing in, in
as I again Eskimo-kiss
the small violet.

iii

An Eskimo-kiss
for the violet ... reflecting
on the love I miss.

These Gifts

Beside the photograph of my wife and children –
an aquarium bowl with green weed ribboning

through the clear water supporting four small fishes,
four fin-waving, glass-bumping, pebble-gulping koi,

and a slim-necked white vase with a gold daffodil
bending on its tall stem to torchlight my papers –

these wonders as I ponder and pen at my desk,
these gifts of gladness from the Eternal Goodness

whose breath is our being, whose love is our longing.

Haijin and Violet

I. Suggestion

i

A haijin suggests
to a little mauve violet –
try this one for size.

ii

Oh Master Basho,
did you know you'd formed a form
just right for violets?

iii

Rescued by haiku –
a little violet smothered
in its own foliage.

II. Reflection

i

The master's violets
held in haiku and haiga –
still strangely touching.

ii

Across the centuries
the same sweet flowers – Basho's
haiga of violets.

iii

About these violets –
conveying to the knowing
a breath of Basho.

III. Realisation

i

A haiku moment –
suddenly realising God
has violets in mind.

ii

These divine violets –
who'd have thought the Almighty
imagined such things?

iii

These violet violets –
more outstanding haiku from
the Divine Haijin.

The Gravity of the Slight

Gravity can grab
even a thing as slight as
a dragonfly wing.
Look, the end of the still blade
is dipping towards the earth.

Tuft

Tufting from
its enamel elytra

the ladybird's wings

imperfectly folded
after flight

Gossamer Web

i

So sensitive
it could detect solar winds –
gossamer web.

ii

Little spider
that web couldn't hold even
a mosquito!

iii

A spinnaker
to take me away – the web
I'm blowing on.

Flywire

i

Summer morning –
a humid breeze grates itself
through the flywire.

ii

Jerky, erratic –
a spider searching the grid
of the flywire screen.

iii

The flywire screen
gives a matt finish to the scene
the window frames.

Disturbance

Again from the corner
of my writing-room window

that sticky, ripping sound
as a plump spider scampers

in pursuit of some purpose
through and over its web –

that tacky, tearing sound
like Velcro unfastening.

Alighting

Clamping itself
to the slim shaft of the now
swaying arrow
bamboo, a grey butcherbird
outside my writing window.

Wheatbelt Willy-Willy

No matter how the fingers stretch
and splay, there remains
a depression in the palm of the hand.

Just so the sparsely stubbled
wheatbelt paddock dips
indecisively beyond the far fence.

And in the hollow, the wind
is dancing like a gypsy, whirling
in her red skirts, her auburn hair.

Great Northern Highway

i
Pilbara highway –
a cattlegrid grips my tyres
as if in warning.

ii
Suddenly, black
Brahman bulls on the black road
in the blackness.

iii
Over a hundred –
so fast the standing bulls came
at us in the night!

iv
Rubber burning –
the smell of it long after
my hard braking.

Focus

i

With my camera
I untangle the beauty –
Pilbara landscape.

ii

The camera lens
framing and fixing the land
oblong by oblong.

iii

In the viewfinder,
defined by being confined,
boab and boulder.

Sighting

On visiting the Bull Ranges with a traditional landowner

Pluck out the detecting eye,
break off the pointing finger,
shut up the exclaiming cry –
if only somehow I could!

But it's too late to stifle
myself now or stop my friend,
who snatches up his rifle
and follows swiftly after

the wallabies I sighted,
the small wild rock wallabies
whose survival I blighted
simply because I saw them

and cried aloud, delighted.

Aboriginal Women

Imagine women
sitting by those worn hollows
on the granite slab
grinding seeds, adding water
from the rockpool, and laughter.

Depressions

i

Long ago, women …
the rockpool rock remembers
their grass-seed grinding.

ii

Grooves in the granite …
the grinders, the grinding stones,
the ground seeds are gone.

iii

Strangely depressing –
these depressions in the stone
from bygone grinding.

Overheated

In the shrinking pool,
a dying marron, its shell
jacked up like the cab
of a semitrailer with
an overheated engine.

Heat

19 January 1991, third day of the Gulf War, Desert Storm

I wake exhausted from the heat.
Dreams will not drift to me again
today. Resentfully, I rise, dress
and leave the house. The street

is empty, evacuated by sleep.
It's barely six but already the sun
is rising above the rooftops
like a rocket with kills to keep.

From one house, news of the war
– that earnest, incessant drone
of the announcer's voice! – sorties
from a radio through an open door.

Perhaps the Great Assize
swirls in the dusts of the Desert
Storm. Halfway round the world
warplanes are rising to the skies.

Feather

A cockatoo tail feather
spearing the pine needles
as if marking a sacred site:

I take it home for my son.
Soon he'll want to play Indians.
And then he'll want a gun.

Black Cockatoos

As they like all creatures
came originally from Mind,
not matter, the cockatoos
are part of the supernatural.

And hearing a large flock
croak and snarl and creak
in the crowns of the gums,
I realise just how easily

a man could mistake them
for black spirits, demented
and dreadful, if he did not
know that 'black' as a state

of the heart belongs sadly
solely to humans and demons.

Twilight with Corellas

i

Corellas settle
with flutes and toots of gladness
in twilit white gums.

ii

In residue light
the gorge resounds with roosting
corella voices.

iii

Softly at nightfall
along the pools of the gorge
white corellas call.

Breakdown, Eneabba, WA

Etched faintly by the light of the stars
the track stretches straight before us,
mile upon endless, empty mile.

We are too weary, and it is too cold, to talk.
We listen to the grind of the gravel
to maintain a rhythm as we walk.

And all the while the wind is up –
the wind is up all the while! – flaying
across the flat of the land.

Light clouds drift in from the west
to weaken the constellations.
Ahead of us, at the edge of the world,

not far from where we are bound,
a diffusion of light dilutes the darkness.
It grows and fills a corner of the sky.

Then unbelievably the moon
bursts above the disc of the earth,
bright with its borrowed light.

Beautiful! I try to comfort myself.
But the whiteness gouges my eyes
and the wind is still up with its whip.

Sestina on a Journey

The road exhales in the cold night. Planes of fog
refract away from the swift approach of my lamps.
I rarely travel the middle ground: mostly I'm alone.
But tonight the white lines are my standard
as they strafe towards me like a broken cry
for battle. I fight to believe some things are good.

There are clever men who claim that good
is merely the flip of a mythical coin. In the fog
no one cares to call the toss. Earnestly they cry,
'It's wrong to believe in wrong!' They dim the lamps
of conscience. They attack the High King's standard.
They strive to convince us that we are alone.

I journey inwardly accompanied, outwardly alone.
I know this is essential and essentially good.
The Spirit of the Lord will raise a standard
against them when the foemen come in like a fog.
We live and die in the light of chosen lamps.
We choose the voice with which we cry.

From the swamplands there is a cacophonous cry,
accompanied always by echoes, never alone.
The marsh men urge us to smash all lamps
and set the world aflame. They croak that good
is a god who plays mouse in the fog
of our thoughts. They stand against a standard.

The journey requires the choice of a standard
or we veer into darkness with barely a cry.
A distant car is a nimbus in the fog.
It is reassuring to know we are alone
together in this obscurity – it is good
to see the beam or flicker of other lamps.

It appears dawn is breaking just before lamps
lift above the heft of a hill: night's standard
falls to light's banner. All hope it is good,
though few await or anticipate a celestial cry.
We are responsible to no one if we are alone.
We are tangled in the netting of the fog.

Few lament the lack of lamps, still fewer cry
at the loss of every standard. Autonomous and alone
we seek a collective good before we collide in the fog.

Train to Wyong

for Peter Kocan

I had thought the journey was merely the price
of arrival – a tedium that would deliver me
to my destination. But through the window I see
my mistake. The hills and the forests entice

interest. This is my country but not my place,
so every sight is a deja vu. Gum trees splice
their limbs together. The train cuts a slice
through a hill. Ferns wave from the rockface.

The track touches the curve of a gorge that falls
steeply to water. A sudden sense of space
and height. Hills again. Not even man can deface
this beauty. After the tunnels, the huge halls

of light. Fluted with drill holes, the hills
blasted for the motorways look like the walls
of ruined castles. The railway bridge sprawls
across an estuary where yachts shake their quills.

I gaze out, accept each gift the journey brings.
Too soon my station comes. The train slows, stills.
On the siding, like a symbol for the world's ills,
a pigeon flutters pathetically with hurt wings.

Preening

A dove, preening
in the leafless almond tree …
and lifting from
its breast, a little feather
that had discomforted it.

Heron Walking

i

A sense of suspense –
the heron beside the stream
suspends its next step.

ii

Still to be put down –
the backward-bending leg
of the grey heron.

iii

Ponderous heron –
placing its claw precisely
where it projected.

Happiness

A small green bird is hopping
up the grey trunk of a river gum.
The tree leans toward the water.
A duck floats on its reflection.

The climbing bird knocks a fleck
of bark into the water. The duck
inspects it then paddles away.
The Chinese poet Tu Fu wrote,

'After the laws of their being
all creatures pursue happiness.'
Watching the birds, the dragon-
flies, it occurs to me that Fu

is quite wrong. Apart from man,
all creatures simply *are* happy.
No duck ends the day with regret.
We alone aspire to something

Other. And we alone fall short.

Gesture

As a woman might
thrust out her palms, fingers splayed,
in a quick gesture
of warding – so the landing crow
shied in shock at the sight of me.

My Daughter's Rabbit

As I recall the death of my daughter's rabbit,
it occurs to me just how callous I have become.
I was not a witness, but my wife told me
it was sudden, a sudden frothing and kicking,
then stillness. Oh death, ugliness becomes you!

Which rabbit? The black one, her favourite.
The one she kept in the bird cage and let out
on a leash. I remember now, weeks later,
how the next morning I saw her in the kitchen,
my youngest daughter, subdued, puffy-eyed.

'Yes,' I said. (Did I hug her?) 'Mum told me.
I'm sorry.' And that was it. That was all
I felt for the rabbit – and worse, for my girl.
I remember the white rabbit I had as a boy,
the one a cat mauled. I recall my tender heart.

What is happening to me? Lord, have mercy!
When she gets home from school, my daughter,
I'm going to say to her, 'Show me the grave,
the grave where you buried your rabbit.'
I'm going to ask and look, I swear it, swear it!

Renewal

It is spring again
and though, Lord, I am jaded
I see everywhere
the sweet signs of renewal
and my spirit sighs,
sighs in hope of the new earth –
oh, birds cosy eggs,
lambs add liveliness to flocks
and the trees put on their frocks!

Search

Just above the sea
of leaves in the violet patch –
one purple flower
like a periscope searching
for any approach of spring.

Lawn

It looks like
the definition of
neglect, that lawn.

Yet inexplicably
today the tenants
are drawn to it.

He worships with
a weeding fork,
while nearby she

blesses with a hose.

Chimes

Sawn into tubing
the giant bamboo cannot
speak anymore in
susurrations ... instead it chimes
from its danglings in dull dongings.

Wind and Tree

i

When the spring wind
slaps the almond tree
petals spurt from its branches
like sparks from a windrow.

ii

The wind in summer
unfastens neither leaf
nor fruit. Nor does it fluster
the feasting parrots.

iii

Last night the autumn wind
took the almond tree
as a fox takes a chicken
and shakes its feathers off.

iv

Soon the winter wind
will lash the latticed limbs
but the tree will barely notice,
having nothing to lose.

Noughts and Crosses

i

A cyclone-wire gate
becomes for zebra finches
a tick-tack-toe grid!

ii

Which is X, which O –
finches in the cyclone wire
playing tick-tack-toe?

Perch

Where the currawongs
perch in the snottygobble
to inspect the ripening

berries, the branch has
lost its plump bark and become
slim and red as a raw bone.

Statues

i

Bird or statue –
that stone or feather heron
in the farm yard?

ii

A nervous glance
betrays a beating heart in
the heron statue.

iii

Getting closer –
the white-faced heron and I
playing statues.

Delay

If I get going
as I should, when again will
I hear things as sweet
as these swallow-twitterings
from the wires in the street?

Attention

Their adoration
would rise if only they could
attract attention –
the donkey orchids herding
in the jarrah trees'
leaf litter and light shadows
in mute auburns and yellows.

Worship

Released from
Sunday School
the children

are chasing
grasshoppers
on the lawn.

Jumbled and
jolly, they
creep and jump.

Leaping up,
my soul is
snatched midair.

Grounding a Grasshopper

'If you don't want it
to hop away,' the child said
as she caught again
the grasshopper near her knee,
'you just pull its legs off ... see?'

Afterthought

i

Lifting her foot,
craning her neck – the woman
holding the eggs.

ii

Little off balance –
the woman by the chook run
pondering her sole.

iii

Scraping away –
the woman beside the hens,
scratching away.

iv

As if moon-walking –
the woman holding the wire
of the chicken coop.

Impossible

Impossible to guess what went
through her mind when she dressed
to go shopping this morning,

that tubby woman in the tight
T-shirt with eye-glasses stencilled
over the bulge of her bosom

framing the words (LOOK)—(AT ME).

Little Hollow

Fill it with water,
that little hollow at base
of her throat, fill it
with water for an eyebath,
and rinse in the loveliness.

Painting in the Painting

Margaret Olley's oil on canvas, Girl Sewing

Is it to fill a space on the wall
or in the girl, that painting
in the painting of a *Girl Sewing*?

See it? Above her bowed head,
a small bluish square with black slap-
dash strokes coalescing as boats.

Prow, gunnel, mast – three vessels.
Onboard one, I suspect, a boy,
trawling the heart of the sewing girl.

Drawing a thread through her cloth,
she imagines a line in the creases
of his fingers. 'Oh, Johnny, John!'

she murmurs. 'Let me be your sea.
I have waves and a harbour. Oh,
come back, and be a mariner to me!'

Boat

The new boat. I bought it mostly
for my boy, who at fifteen has become
black and thunderous. An aluminium
dinghy with ten horses behind it –
something to interest him, something
to give us something in common.
And yesterday it did. I swear
he was almost happy as we launched
the boat in the bay for the first time.
Our small craft. At full throttle
it sat up and planed! A sensation
of speed, as in a go-kart! Today
he wants to try it by himself.
Sure, I say, stepping to the shore.
Why not? I push the prow out to sea.
He pulls the cord and powers away,
heads out without looking back.
The dinghy skips over the light chop,
going out and out. I watch him,
the boy I've not loved nearly enough.
My son, who grows bigger in my heart
even as he grows smaller in my eyes.
He is on the sea, going directly
away from me. And I notice now
what I should have noticed before –
the cloudbank on the horizon.
Black clouds coming in. And the boy
still going out! I watch and watch,
willing him to turn. The boat

no longer glints, having gone
into the shadow of the clouds.
Then suddenly a tear, a bright tear
in the fast encroaching blackness.
And another. No thunder. No rain.
Just lightning, synapsing the dark sky
to the dark sea! The level sea,
on which my son is the highest point.
The empty sea, on which our boat
is the only boat. Lightning! Oh son,
turn back, turn back to the shore!
I beckon and call. But he has gone
too far to see or hear me any more.

Freedom

How foolishly I once thought of freedom.

When my first son was small I sometimes
dreamed of the day I'd be independent

of his demands. At times the chores
of fatherhood hung upon me like chains.

Now he is gone, gone to university, gone
from home – and I am enslaved by loss.

How foolishly I once thought of freedom.

Aftermath

If he were home
we would hardly

know what to say
to each other,

my son and I –
my eldest son.

So why this deep
pang in my heart?

In Dependence

Not until they took
their independence

of me, my children –
not until then, then

did I discover
just how much I am

in dependence, in
dependence on them.

Fathers

Over the air waves,
weeping, a father whose son
killed by negligence
another father's daughter …
Oh, Father – justice, mercy!

Arrival and Departure

for Theodor

I arrived in time to see him die.
I am thankful for that. How bitter
it would be to have been absent
after these weeks in attendance.

There was no last word, no parting
touch or glance – just one final
shuddering gasp. Oh the gaping mouth,
the clouded eyes, the casket chest!

The nurse came, closed his eyelids
and kindly left. I held his hand
briefly, bestowing a little last
warmth against the besetting cold.

After Death

Even those
who doubt
Christ's claim
that

after death
comes judgement

even those
are troubled
by certainty
that

after death
comes forever ...

Should the Marauders Come

She won't go back to the farm
while her husband is in hospital.
She can't go back. She's afraid
of being afraid out there
by herself at night, out there
with only the ducks and the calves
to hear her screech (oh horror,
horror!) should the marauders come.

And who's to say they won't come
for her as they came for that man
at Manjimup? Three teenagers
at the farmhouse door with hearts
like fists, fists with knives.
Three robbers who stopped short
of murder because they thought
the stabbed man was stabbed dead.

One in a million, of course. But
who's to say that of the next million
she's not the next one? Besides,
another marauder is waiting already.
Those empty boots, that unwrinkled
sheet! *My beloved!* The presence
of his absence is stalking through
the house. She knows it, knows it!

Don't try to counsel or correct her.
She is right to be afraid
of being afraid out there alone.
Let her stay in town at the motel.
There are noises there to remind her
she is not alone in the world.
And people nearby who will hear,
perhaps even help, if she should scream.

Night Noises

An owl on the wing,
a fox on the prowl – what, oh,
what lurking horror
tore those noises from the throat
of that rabbit in the night?

Prayer

Oh, for my mother in her pain,
Almighty and all-loving Lord,
I come to plead with you again.

For years her body's been a bane
That's put all gladness to the sword:
Oh, for my mother in her pain!

Too much misery makes a stain
To black all light and block all laud:
I come to plead with you again.

Today at least relieve the strain
And give reprieve as a reward,
Oh, for my mother in her pain.

I know there is no other Name.
Despite the fact my faith is flawed,
I come to plead with you again.

Although my many sins maintain
That I deserve to be ignored –
Oh, for my mother in her pain
I come to plead with you again!

Pain Haiku

i

My days are not
getting shorter with winter
thanks to this pain.

ii

This pain, it seems so
merciless and meaningless –
it seems so, this pain!

iii

Like a fine haiku
the pain occupying me is
so present and pure.

iv

I think of Shiki
writing haiku and tanka
in spite of the pain.

Relief

It is, I suppose,
the sort of thing watchmen felt
as from the towers
they saw their foe lift the siege –
this relief I feel
as the drugs settle a truce
and the pain starts to retreat.

Shadow

Again the shadow
of an unseen bird crosses
a patch of sunlight
pooled in the shade of the tree
whose branches arch over me.

Being Bamboo

i

The shakuhachi
remembers its bamboo self –
oh, the hollowness!

ii

With or without
breeze the dangling bamboo chimes
are stopt and mute.

iii

One as a wind-chime,
one as a flute – the bamboos
excelling themselves.

Pod

Split and twisted
but still paired

a dried acacia pod

like the double
helix of a gene

Brimming

A cup on a cross-
beam in the carport,

a grass cup covered
with a cobweb gauze –

the nest some goodness
has filled to the brim

with wagtail hatchlings
that lift wobbling heads

above the low rim
and gape with gladness

each time their parents
return with insects,

not to mention twit-
chings and chatterings!

End of Day

We pass the cows on their way
  to the milking shed
and the farmer's easing hands.

Frogs are gladly chorusing
  like little gibbons
in the dark reeds by the soak.

We cross the fallow paddock
  to a stand of trees
surrounded by burnt bracken.

The fire has found a refuge
  in the deep hollow
at the base of a dead tree.

In the absence of rabbits
  I slip back the bolt
and lay the rifle aside.

My sons collect sticks and roots
  to stoke the jarrah
tree's self-consuming furnace.

A pair of pygmy bats hunt
  and even dogfight
in the twilight and the smoke.

Did you bring the bullet, Dad?
  I toss the cartridge
that misfired into the fire.

We run for cover and cheer
  in shock and joy at
the expected explosion.

We are happy together
  my small sons and I
here at the dark end of day.

SONGS SUL G

Kevin Gillam

KEVIN GILLAM's books of poetry include *Other Gravities* (Sunline Press, 2003) and *Permitted to Fall* (Sunline Press, 2007). He has had poems in *The Best Australian Poems 2006*, *The Best Australian Poems 2008*, and *The Best Australian Poetry 2006*, and broadcasts on ABC Radio Poetica (featured poet 2007). Kevin Gillam has won numerous awards for his poetry including the Woorilla Poetry Prize, the Trudy Graham Biennial Literary Award, the Manly Fellowship of Australian Writers Poetry Award, The Reason-Brisbane Poetry Prize, and many others. Kevin is currently employed as Director of Music at Christchurch Grammar School and works as a freelance cellist and orchestral conductor.

ACKNOWLEDGEMENTS

Journals in which these poems have been published include: *Overland, Island, Meanjin, Heat, Southerly, Linq, Wet Ink, Westerly, Australian Book Review, Famous Reporter, Southern Review, Australian Literary Review, Tamba, Woorilla, Stylus, Leaf Press, Eureka Street, The Mozzie, Small Packages, Unusual Work, Page Seventeen, FourW, Idiom, Sidewalk, Five Bells, POAM, Prospect, Blue Giraffe, Sitelines* and *Etchings*.

CONTENTS

twelve-bar blues

you begin stooped, growling, gravelly,
at home here, schmoozing upwards, licking
sideways at augmented fourth, glissing
and caressing the minor seventh

then falling to third, your voice sweeter,
less grunged, scuffing hearts, caramel hued

for home, gum leaves and pedal steel, whiff
of being in front bar carpet for

the wail of lost orphan drenched top notes,

the leaking, licorice left in sun,

the return, notes bent, borrowed, stolen,
gruff and under, shimmying back in

the necessary

the necessary leap,
hands in fiction, praying
to dun earth. necessary

ponder, mind spent on
tessellating. necessary scent

of rosemary, blood and
order. necessary trust in
tome and tongue? necessary

stained wonder.
necessary still

songs sul G

dark hums. the air furs. you're giddy with it,
drunk on ungravity. you hear

plainsong unravelling, smell earth organic
and forgiving, sense ecstatic stillness.

black swarms and dances, has you as one,
paints you out and salmon gums stand

with breath held, mooned backs turned away.
sky purple blooded, your hands on mound

of stomach tight with tomorrow, membranes alive
with unreadable promise. china cabinet night,

all places in their plates, all mothers
stacked in velvet, rubbed of stained pasts.

warmth pressing, once salted fiction, now
amniotic-held truth. wood amongst wood,

this lute of you, fretless, songs sul G.
because and should don't grow here, shredding winds

not felt. breeze rewrites the bracken.
mopoke sounds. waters

once

on wheel of sky, at
whim of wind, clouds making then
unmaking themselves

unseeing rain plays
to itself, hears 'when' in wet-
ness, skin of betweens

Venus, up early,
bulleting the tarpaulin
of thinking man's blue

after Sydney storms
broken umbrellas strewn, the
guise of life in death

moon up there in your
sixpence world, do you too see
us as moulded coin?

a history of breathing

opens with eucalyptus leaf,
a rubbing, and through the
laid down bustle of a blunt HB
veins curving edgewards present
as elegant maths

on page six a colour plate of sea,
blur of spume, insistent brine.
there is no convoluting here,
there are no clean lines, just the
endless suck of wave on sand,
the tug, the susurration

hessian sky (centre pages),
pegged just beyond reason,
taut in all hours but those
gifting drip. tent of thought,
call it that, blue or grey to
chaperone mood. and plump cumulus,
smear of cirrus stencilled on –
shadow denied for disbelievers

skin, chapter fifteen, keeps doubt
from leaking. unblemished, but then
scalpelled, sutured, a wallet of hours.
'dermis is diary' – that line
has you hooked. yes, drop a tail
but pores won't keep the stories in

one page, the last, for wonder.
ear against a dying paperbark,
yes, that's you, the tree crickling,
crickling out its name.
and your lungful of what if

gliss

back then crows went by that name and in church
their stretched 'farks' near on stole both the creed and
Lord's prayer and the roof was sheep ribs and Mum
said she'd sinned but I knew that was a fib
and me? I was off in chase of thrill back

when I was of years to push peas to the
edge of plate of day, the world of yard then
split 'tween couch and bush, tamed and lush where on
a Sat. flames frilled and ants and bark and us
danced drunk on the ooze of now 'til called in,
tucked in, spoon fed prayer, let of doubt, taught of
strings that bound us here and kept Him up and

back there first was scent of soaps in the two
Nans, one rose, one mint and leaf and from then
cut grass and dove shit and waxed floors and brine,
weed and white bait and dried tree sap on bow
hairs then the kick, smell of morphed air in room
of none as rays bored bone to mute and still
and me? I was lost to stun and angst back

where that crack, that black hole peeled then spat me
and in J.S. Bach's Suite in G the first
phrase climbs to a cusp of 8 on 1 and
3, in maths the mean that's gold, found in webs
of orb and crusts of pearl shell and waves and
in my hours, sits high and staked out as 'now'
of a skink's tail as it writes in palm and

lips at cold stream and songs in the key of
rust from swings in park all since air morphed and

back then I was taught the maps of sound then
sense and on these maps there's no nil and staves
start at one so in my first school with the
doves and wax one plus one gave three but there's
the rub, the rhyme, the twitch for 'neath the scabs
and tongue, 'neath the red gift of us, on the
flat side of our neck of days where hands fret
and strum there's blue and be and gliss and leave

when Good Friday comes

mine is a fly-in, fly-out Christ,
sandals off in first class, no hard hat
on site, always home at Christmas

mine is a Festival Director Jesus,
putting lab rats on stage for a
slice of corporate sponsorship pie

mine is a bored-again Saviour,
levitating during PowerPoint presentations,
feeding Nice biscuits to ants at morning tea

mine is a shock-jock Son,
devil's advocate for the right cash offer,
delay button when Good Friday comes

Zens

stepping into the margins of the morning

everything is used – bruised apricots
for jam

propping up a night with procrastination

counting his coins and smiling –
guitar player

scouring the hours for elusive hits of bliss

planning tomorrow while fucking up today

lying in seas named only for their colour

corrugating now's hush with
sheets of grey think

eyeing the rust on your cherry-picker heart

throwing arms wide to Zen with
the Wrangler boy

breathing not, I kiss him, each time
I kiss him

paperbark days

you lead me to stillness. you shell
me and in your mantra of
'stars and mars and moon and dust and
us and stars and mars and' I am
taut and slack and small as should be

you bracken me with now. you
fold me and in modulations
damp and dry I am
tinder and tendril and
template and plundered and none

you sew the sky through me.
you take my paperbark days and
scuff and bluff and bleed and
breathe and leave them as cirrus

the caught

there, on the pickets,
the skink
then not

    you were stilled back then,
                  in the
      light there

the forge-proof exchange
then done,
there framed

    brushed by unthink then,
             just there,
        no 'the'

there, skink on pickets
then you,
the caught

untitled

pissing in the lane,
staining the pickets, unthreading
the rope of ants

each bee

am I swim
ming into
the sky or
the water?
am I wak
ing on the
inside of
dream? do the
goldfish see
me as God
or mother?
does each bee
get to sleep
with the Queen?

Carnaby's

a cloud-scuffed March day goes down among
Salmon Gums, though above the asbestos fence, bouganvillea

and grape are birthing, weighed down by plum-coloured
trumpets and myriads of green baubles. closer by,

from some die-back ridden tuart and maze of fig limbs,
shredding then dropping their excitement over their shoulders,

the black cockatoos murder silence. their cries now have the
same can-opener urgency they had this morning,

and roosting after a day in flight they hold in their throats
the cacophony of now. for them, though the light at sunset

and dawn are of equal intensity, there is a turning earth,
a rising friction. out of the sky they drop,

an unruly squadron, carousing and goading each other on.
just as gum blossoms fill the March air with their scent,

the black cockatoos fill the air with their screeching,
heralding rain, and hinting, perhaps, at something

more ominous. and if humans ceased to exist –
of what matter are humans to black cockatoos? –

there might be one less fig to thieve, one more eon
in which to plunder. if they are God's work

then the hands are steady and skilled, evolution, and the
production line smooth, proven, fate, and there has been

no twist. though we've caged, shot, driven them to near extinction,
they are not ours, and their raucous cries the sound of reason

dead trees

prefer wounds to sores.
like to keep my thoughts clear of
eruptions. see the

fig as the god of
now, flowering inside. press
my ear to dead trees

tin, bricks and jarrah

house number in red,
dribbling like blood across the
galvanised gangrene

outside wall of chook
run and dunny, cake icing
crumbling between dreams

pickets bleached grey and
rickety, more idea
than reality

the jetty of you

if you were to lie here long enough,
let the moon do its work,
let tide and salt and wind lick your stories,
gulls thieve your last commas,
just you then, the full stops, the very stumps
of the jetty of you

if you were to do the forgetting,
allow the sky to scrawl
in cirrus the shaded angst of you,
just you then, taut and wisped
and stretching, all join the dots on blue

if you were, this last time,
to lose North and gravity and being,
just you then, yes, just you

in a hurried life

in a hurried life
you might run your tongue along
a picket fence, learn

about splinters, you
might conclude that the Disprin
pill moon is insol-

uble, you might put
your net around one God, then
get stung by the hive.

in a hurried life
you might find instructions for
grieving, you might have

ration books for dreams.
in a hurried life you might
forget to climb through

the manhole of sky

call it that

crooked history –
call it that – pickets angled
by weather and warp,

the non-fiction of
aged jarrah married through with
honeyed lies of light

black kings

in the shape of moths
come thoughts, in loops that chase light,
and arcs that saw and

jig these loops aren't born
of moths but need, and watt and
amp that dot the joins

gift feed and box to
moths that still as words then cross.
sun smears moon but can't

pluck wings from moths that daub the
boards of snake and rung
then spy the wee eye

and flit to where draughts rest to
wing just the black kings

the space 'tween

you ask me to tell you
of my sky but not use
'blue' and I say it's when
red bleeds from green and I
blink and you're mute and the
space 'tween comes dark in bruise

I ask you to sculpt a truth
in one move and you reach and
with back of hand brush my cheek and
for you it's gift but for me
theft and 'tween is braille not read

we go to sing and seek 'neath
sheep ribs but lip sync creeds then
leave to toss coins in deep wells

the day you came

it was good, and if I'd read my stars
that day I would have found it was
bound to be, would have joined the dots of
fate, the day you slipped through the sky and came
to me. there you stood, glint off sea no
match for your wrap of blue and sheen, charms
strung tight as beads, looped through chat, you so
keen to talk of wings and drift, warm air
that might bid you, yes, on this, the day

you came. me? I was snared, bit, stung, blessed,
floored, found – all of these. and clouds went from
scrawl to sense, leaves danced and blushed then
drew their breath, the moon spun and showed its
not-seen side, the day you came to me

stopping

stopping makes a sound,
offers a plea, drops a hand,
pulls you skyward. stop-

ping lives below the
white sack on the red letter-
box, composes songs

using dust motes. show
closed, stopping warm, beside you
on the ferris wheel

music of sleepers

I need the feather. the cribbed
mouths to feed. humility
lives. we even sing. tarot
of the now. instructions for
leaves. too much unspoken. ease
of last city. the meek in
the sloop. reasons for silence.

evening wings in. woken
through touch. elasticity.
instructions to leave. the fibs
mouthed as creeds. the season for
rhyme. death, humidity. I
feed the ether. music of
sleepers. the now too narrow

and here cats, in here all clouds

you are here for the others.
absolute presence of here.
and here the result, clutching.
here, you see, sound water makes

cats, clouds, cars, heres, opinions.
in here,
'neath rib-caged ceiling

here, in quiet evening.
all journeys end here, now all

clouds scrawl in the cage of here.
it is here, the pinch of dark.
here they pick over the bones

in limbs of silence, here rests,
here to whistle, dark of tomb.
wars end in the home key, here

chromos (for M.L.)

c minor

three black stumps, the rest stained teeth
and clutches of moist thought
pitched on a lid,
Ludwig's four note spade
digging in, digging in

c# minor

the colour of disruption,
bruised and brooding, but then
the healing, a flush of
sunshine and forget,
tonic major

d minor Bach

gifted it to you,
three notes climbing from
dun-coloured earth,
recoiling, faux sunshine,
elegy for the 'morrow

E♭ Major

across ceiling of day
smears of grey, you,
reading fate, feel for rain
but no, it's merely the
moods of Venus shaping

E Major

and for you, partita girl,
bright as an open A,
sonorous as sul G,
never rhyming of course,
thoughts in orange

f minor   your voice atop the sway of
               ćello and brushed snare,
               a graze not forgotten,
               scuffed carpet in the
               front bar of being

G♭ Major   just the blacks, Irving's
               'when I'm calling you' so elegant,
               a tessellation of
               flesh and wood,
               one for each finger

G Major   the garden, this dance of
               bird and bee, third voice
               your keening, or wind-shirred Sound,
               gull, comma cut loose,
               waiting for breathing

A♭ Major   sky unmaking itself,
               the herring in, sewing the water,
               on the jetty a whiff
               of happiness,
               yes, a whiff

a minor   as sulphur-cresteds cry and
               open the can of day,
               as a tongue runs along
               the pickets, as song blurs
               rain and blood

b^b minor   the blackest. Chopin used
a wide-toothed comb,
moved through it Lento,
groomed the decay and silence in
each as much as tone

B Major   in the diary of clean
beginnings you make an entry,
the messenger bird has sung,
on the 'morrow
taste sea

and leave

leave bowls of water for the moon,
take the river's truth and gift it,
see all sides of wet things,
catch the rain and wind in separate hands

leave bowls of wind for the hands,
catch the moon's truth and wet it,
see all gifts in rain things,
take the river and water to separate sides

weave water and moon,
slake the river of gifts,
seed the truth with rain,
shake the river of separate lands

sleeve the moon,
wake the river,
sift rain,
hatch and leave

from the verandah

rag-washed sky,
tin, light and dreaming,
hills stubbly, straw yellow,
Sunday hunkered down

cicadas, hum of aircon,
thongs slap atop gravel,
hint of breeze, but no

powerlines, staves unplayed,
leaves matt finished

Godless, waiting

last bits

moon tugs at the
wet in me. earth

lays claim to the
pelt of me. a

crow waits to thieve
the night from me.

the cross gives a
glow to the guilt

in me. time winks
at the angst in

me. and you? you're
there with shirt box

and pins for the
last bits of me

seeing all fish

if Jesus was
a swimmer he'd
be you, blue flip-
pers for sandals,
sinewed torso
arrowing the
surf, bearded lips
sucking at now,
at one in the
sea's wilderness,
smoothing the thrill
and ripple, you,
seeing all fish,
dreaming of loaves

exact coinage

we're lined up (as you do)
on a Saturday,
each with our handful of
sixpack or Cabernet Merlot promise,
mind's full of justify
(it *is* Saturday, not thinking,
of course, about the
Escher-logic required
for the morrow)

she's in front of me
clutching two cans of Export,
cheeks ruddy and corrugated,
puppet eyelids,
then, at the counter,
a slurry of lips, words, sense
but she's got exact coinage for
her booze and pack of
Winnie Golds, she's got
her night sorted

passacaglia

me I'm out scouring back lanes for
moments of leaving – raven's feather, at
certain angles indigo, rubbing
palms across fretting brickwork, brailling
belief, beyond gums, cumulus
dolloped on the horizon – all seethes of
waiting, tilting, shutters of a mind –

straw fashioned from fingernail, the
idea of flight, clay and sand and
water and think and infinity, one
fistful of dream dropped long before care
and thought got tangled, touch the one trick,
nothing so still, nothing so present,
pulling me through tenses, was to is

takes

shake the tree of doubt. bait
the hour with now. ache
is body song. notate
the talk of clouds. take
longer strides. equate?
yes, try to. mistakes
make catchy riffs. fate
won't hear you shout. spake
once then listened thrice.
create on steady decks.
slake sounds like it feels.
weight of wonder? quake
is best left for gods.
exclamate! exclamate!

felt more than saw

in the church felt more than saw,
creed through chest bone, throbb-
ing of hymn the length of me

in the dark church scent of book
and sigh of prayer cush-
ion and sheep rib sky stole me

in the blood-dark church I passed
the cup and mouthed be-
lief and stood clean and empty

the colour of disruption

without the servo and hotel it's Spain,
somewhere out, somewhere South.
it's the gates and spire that catch you,
jagging on the remembered,
recasting blue as elsewhere.
even the eucalypts,
tangling skyward behind the clump of
monastery buildings, seem exotic.
two monks stand out front –
ravens come to mind, but then no,
ravens don't move in pairs

you have to be here, pulled to this place by
the colour of disruption. Salvado too,
drawn here by order and zeal,
by a desire to shed a dark light.
there is a wide silence here,
many bar lines through something rubbed out.
years have only added more staves

stepping from the car, heat's shimmer and
brickwork come at you in stripes.
bells, and you're back in night's dormitory,
nailed to the hour. quick fingers,
urgent breaths, lips on the burrs of
flannelette sheets. well-muscled Jesus
waits elsewhere

inside the chapel air intincted with
prayers of too many, light stained,
as if from somewhere beyond the sun.
you gently slide into a pew, running your
hands along worked smoothness of
ritual and creed. swarm of mind moves to
the cartooned disciples along the wall, until
one bell chimes the quarter hour.
outside, black cockatoos arrive,
raucously shredding the almond trees.
first rains are due. soon five months' dust
will slurry the pools

in the midst of the service you look up,
see thin gods writhing in a painted sky.
and thinking – difficulty of precision,
instincts hidden beneath the drape of black,
ravens and confusions of choice and anonymity.
clouds of incense leave you sweating in Sunday best

it has travelled with you this ulcered chant,
ruptured your hours, sang as round as
you sat with pillows.
you unpack your case, but then repack,
for there will be no salve here

night road. low hum. high beam. no sky.
you, lost in the gossip of tyres and wet bitumen,
you, catcher and shaper, painter, etcher,
lost in the 'morrow.
what hair of brush for a waning moon?
width of chisel for shame?

the depth of a day

she sits, in her plenty,
in her squalor. behind her
the dog wheezes in sleep,
bar heater ticks arthritic.
behind her rests another
vacant day, a cloudless sky
when keening for rain.
she's thinking about that,
about what's behind, in front

In Remembrance
Timothy Arthur Boyd

do we move through hours
or stand still as hours glide
around us? who snips the
deadheads of spent time?

1981–2005
To my hazel-eyed one

clasping her hands, she notices
the blueness of veins snaking
across bone. why blue
and not red? she thinks

War took you young.
God keeps you close.

from beyond the window a
. car door slams, a car starts.
life's about that. closing
and going. she remembers
thinking that before

Mum

'life's about making knots in
the frayed but same-coloured ends.'
she says this out loud, nodding
to herself, nodding to the
uniformed young face in the frame,
knowing that she's felt
the depth of a day

on grass

always taken it as given
that I'd die outside,
on solid ground, on grass,
thought it might be flames
that took the box of me
or some herd, free of fences,
on the graze

no, flies first, a Good Friday
Catholic congregation of them,
beetles gnawing silence,
ravens to finish,
gifting my sinew,
ventricles, my commas
to sky

prayer cushions

under a therapist's sky you glide the lane of
your making. besides the flamboyant swirl

of graffiti tag on a garage door and waft of
cigarette smoke, it's as it was yesterday.

each afternoon this lane is yours for the painting.
you dream in tongues here, scour the cosmos

of bitumen, leave, return peeled, segmented,
reassembled. the sky is crumpled tin foil,

not yours – you don't do ceilings or looking up.
in veiled light you're back then, selecting a pew,

parasite on the ribs of something itself parasitic.
if prayer cushions were to speak. imminent

this question – when is now? as a child at the piano,
thumb pressed C on the beat of now. in the lane

now is the fences and fretting brickwork that wait
for the rub and brush of your mood. in your hours

a clock without hands. this morning, volts strapped
to your temples. waking, light crepuscular, lane

or nave? reply leathered, insistent, now is then

a kind of archaeology

old and grubby Gods were mine,
aren't now. mine are slivers,
more side than top.

I don't wake to crickets
nor coat-hangered thoughts.

this morning, when I realised
the house was burning

there were others, hymns of them,
a glimmer of dawning.

'for rent and a small stipend' –

signs – a kind of archaeology.

my footsteps find a rhythm,
black rags of raven pass overhead,

a sense of pale sadness forms.
disliking stillness

the angle of feathers

the bird articulates death better,
full stop on the footpath,
two feathers raised skyward,
reminders

walking past the child stares, mouths death,
can't sound it. something
about the angle of feathers
speaks for him

sooty sky

these are black days. mine a sooty
sky. grit falls with rain. thinking wet,

won't catch. black days are these. these
days aren't those. past tense a

varnish. these minutes splinter. pierce
hands of fate. future pain racked. black

days these are. pills bleach a.m.
p.m. coma grey. these are black days

tenné

orange inside your eyelids,
you make no futures, believe

in too few. smeared far above
last days of scab, summer cloud.

you'd like to feel the absence
of fingers, to know the far-

off blindness of a body.

'but we're all missing something' –

you hear your father in you,
his exhaling. a bag of

oranges waits, bundle of
suns. you wait for gravity,

the pull of something closer,
attractions unpeeled, unsung

from freo

it's the jaundiced streetlight. it's the
black-lined lung of harbour. it's
the hum of unthinking. it's the bill-
boards screaming. it's Friday bleeding.
it's the unsilence. it's a fresh
tongue of tar. it's the whiff of poss-
ibility. it's tail lights in
soft focus. it's a bottle-top

sky. it's the unsilence. it's un-
seens and scheming. it's the strip
and neon hit. it's the smeared mirror's
lie. it's the unsilence. it's the
lips of driveway. it's the first
sip of stopping. it's the silence

wet brush

you lose yourself, wake,
lose the lost. you've pangs

for the warmth of else,
a kind of prang in

a plot you won't know.
blurred now, sly work of

pills. they did tell you
that it won't be etch

or fine shades of H.
B. that will take you,

no, just the back/forth
of wet brush, slow touch,

an ache that births hue,
blood that dries to dust

the anaesthetist's share

am breathing in sunshine, in silence,
in an afternoon still as regret.

you're not with me, off and not,
on the tongue, all that's unsaid.

we are vespers, we are all sung,
we have been out here, bush-fired sunsets,

cinders of betweens. and there is you,
ghost limb, collection bowl, a throb,

a guilt, a staining, as if am
moth-wing fingered, as if have been

mouthing hymns, forgetting, like
losing North, surrendering the

anaesthetist's share. but am breathing out
fret and make-believe to this

smashed up sky, to twigs on doorsills,
am setting traps.

but, turning left, moving right,
with the hum of wires, this seagull heart,

words long as notes, not yet
at the crossing of leaving/longing,

in the could of did. this smeltered now,
blood and time and water,

or, perhaps, the weight of silence,
bar lines through hours unplayed.

perhaps bark has ceased book-ending.
where are the small deities

for frail thinking, the lakes for intincting?
where sits the drum of scalded leaves,

your gun-powdered maps and creeds?

now this

none flow
window sifting feeble morning light
here
unthere
no rush, no push
can hear birds
and then remember
white-yellowness
theories of skin
losing North
now this
two doves cooing a tone apart
B to A
none flow

for some reason

for him, numbers were his plug, as
sometimes (and he'd read this, man of
reason that he was),
he felt the bath-water spiral
(didn't everyone?) towards madness,
inviting the sweet collapse, gifts of
meander, violent shake, up/down
in/out of jigsaw box

some numbers looped, spun in this man of
reason, and, fully given over, he
didn't fight, didn't kick, couldn't, just
invited, in from the cold, hot
meal, fire and time, in,
in from the cold came his numbers

braille of tide

atop the rigging
of mind sits a nest where an
eye might spot, dolloped

on the horizon,
the island of Bliss or the
treacherous Bleak Reef.

uncharted waters,
like the Dead Sea, lead to nest
evacuation.

in persistent fog
the nest goes unmanned, and mind
shifts by braille of tide

on crooked sea

melody and silence,
we began like this,
thin lips on a crooked sea

froth and angst, susurrations,
our rush became riff,
melody then silence

should've read the scrawl of sea-
weed, heard the talk from
thin lips in crooked sea

gulls hovered, tore at
phrase and stave, defleshed us,
melody into silence

now's quarrel – whose oceans whose?
no dotted lines, only
crooked lips, thin sea

the jetty planks lie splintered,
one tern waiting, mute,
melody gone silent,
wooden lips on crooked sea

pylon

a groyne-walled sea, the surf's swift slap,
the quiet wind's cut, your concrete torso of etch

and grey, melding into froth, a lull,
your resilience, value of iconography.

do not become fashion, do not become
cloned, do not let shire safety wire

deny us your landing. today, drawing pin
in brine, launch pad for board-shorted

esteem, wet thumb in breeze, can paint you
in only this place. proposed now?

laughed down ... 'on what precedent?
... for what purpose?' at this hour

welcomed by surrounds, festooned in weed,
bricked by mussels. not lonely, not stoic,

not flotsam in wait of shore.
whipped by sou-westers, rocking-horse manes

on waves, spume, one gull in hover
and you, watching, fixed in your station.

evening glides silently in, horizon line
begins mending, and you wait,

stylus on an unplayed sea. tonight
herring will sew themselves around you,

tide will sing, and tomorrow, another
will swim to you, climb, jump and fly

those sweet things

and I'm up to put an end to night and make
a start to day and you say with your mouth
full of oats that you've found a rhyme for the
fruit with peel and pith and pips and you say this
with an oat on your lip and you say its those

sweet things you suck when you've got a cold but I
say I don't know what you mean and then you

get peeved and sulk and say you'll take your words
and hide them and not let me play and I say
how 'bout a rhyme for the hue that's more dark than
mauve and that makes you stop the chew and muse and

this is our start of day and this is the start
to all our days and its weird how we find
rhymes for fruit and hues but can't find rhyme in us

Tourettic

my words are miscarriages,
the room maps the blood
as symptoms find their opening

she writes … 'the myth of locks',
asks me to read aloud … 'the moth of licks',
words as miscarriages

a duffle bag of tongue clicking,
whistling, floor tapping, rapid head turns,
symptoms finding their opening

the urge to shout in church,
vibrating inside on bones of pew,
my words as miscarriages

I keep my tongue wound in my teeth,
ignore the throbbing in the gullet,
but my symptoms find their opening

I reach for her, tap her shoulder,
let fly a staccato burst of caresses
then words as miscarriages,
symptoms finding their opening

the twelfth year

I will lose my
shadow. I
will give it
up in
pieces. I
will read the
scrawl of cirrus.
I will
tessellate my
needs. I will
forget,
in the twelfth
year of many,
your name

when the sea

when the sea was
dark and rough
it was my
feet that did
the speaking

sold it to me,
no deals,
no interest

waves in-breathing
making speech
suddenly deeper

my feet
on about this
rare cold stopping

act I

it was a night when
all was as it should have been
but then I dropped my

script and said what I'd
learned, what I felt and what I
could see and then you

struck a match and in
that heat and fret you shed a
skin, you dropped your tail

aged rain

the afternoon mind. the af-
ternoon moved. afternoon

mooned. a trick of light? trick of
sight? truth of pill? a gift of

mirage? god couldn't manage?
fate couldn't fence in? you then,

one of a deck? you then,
diamond or hearts? the unsmiling

jack? guileless, guilty of naught?
guileless, one of a flush? caught,

guilty, blushing, framed? from the brush
of aged rain. from the window,

you, paned. window, rafters
swooning. the afternoon moved

dead apple

propped. no news. not
drinking. smirr of

forty watts. floor
polish. dead apple.

with the moth. bit
smeared. kookaburras

and Stravinsky.
bit smudged. yellowed

music. stained breves.
skirting. untaughts.

bit smarmed. stoned on
ostinati.

offered. a bit.
night. no exchange

Wednesday's child

so I take me to
river and toss you to sky
and go into soft

focus and find that
Wednesday's child isn't always
full of woe and through

fine mist ('the haar' they
call it here) I see light, I
see moon, I see you

with the bark

bleak takes you to river / late
afternoon / greys and khakis and
dark fawns / day furrowing,

folding in / bracken speaks / you've
no ears /   / black
cockatoos wheeling and
carousing / after rain / scent of
moist earth / bracken tales / bleak
turns the page /   /
light fluorescent now / the river

slick, then rippled / throat song
of magpies on the far bank /
wagtails close, electric /
                        / bleak sits,

blunt on the tongue / dead limbs
crickling / sky pink, sun drowning
elsewhere / as bracken reads its

script / your lines tacit / tuarts
stand, men at the back of
church /   /
the wind, like a dam, everywhere /
sooty light between trees /
                        / cockatoos cry

less urgent / you are tidal, neap /
bleak spilling and pooling /
                                    / the Nor-West
breeze ceases / river is old glass /
                                    / bracken
mouths a gibbous moon / and

light's gone to ash and black
cockatoos moving / bleak sutures
its wound /
                        bracken licking it
clean /
                        / all the birds now

– ravens, warblers, wrens –
cacophony /
                        / the
smell of wet leaf /
                                    /
river seeping both sides of

its name /
                        / you? /
                                    /moth-winged, with

the bark /
                        / with the bark /
                        / shabby, breathing

etry

the poem's bark, where sap and sense and fret make quickened flow
taught in poetry, but the word-smiths don't really do that
ash-coloured poem, thieved from midden, smoothed by mind and thumb
rather like poetry without knowing what was coming
rest, letters with poems in them, snapshots of occasions
and watch the penned poems grow brilliantly indistinct
and quote Proust, bring poems from home in air-tight containers

you? yes, you say 'black', poet, but clothed in first person, 'bruised'
a truth told in jest, meant 'poetry' but wrote 'poverty'
people pray to the god of lists, prune poems off roses
and yes beautiful, it's a very poetic picture
but compose best with flutes and schooners, find poems in dregs
was one of those children that wrote horrible poetry
the combination lock click of metaphor in the po

the unwritten blue

remember, in that bruised light – we had dozed in
     the loft of the A-frame, woken
then walked – the tuarts browning skyward, warblers

     and wagtails flitting – you were talking about that book
Life of Pi – then the river, fat, white froth,
     moving left to right as if having been read.

I don't remember who noticed the dead bird first,
     one wing pointing skyward, the unglazed eye.
a bush parrot, burnt red and khaki plumage

     already being reclaimed by bracken. you went to touch it,
saw an ant, pulled away. we were silent then,
     hushed by fate and its casual cruelty,

late afternoon painting in charcoal around us.
     re-tracing our steps, a symphony of drips
and burps from rain and frogs, you on about

     slivered moons and life and fiction and
narrative's tidal pull. it was then,
     in that falter in your voice,

that staccato within legato, that you hinted
     at some loss deeper than sense.
that night, in the warm cusp of the A-frame –

the tropical triangle we called it,
pot-belly below having been going all day –
    you told me about your twin sister who

died at birth, how some days you saw her
    as a bird, flying above and ahead, calls of
kinship or warning, other days as the sky,

    how you'd noticed, out walking and looking up,
that while the gates and letterboxes and gardens stayed still,
    the clouds and unwritten blue moved with you

Blackwood

colour of my shoe, frothing, full up
on winter

and you, crickling out your name

      I imagine you as a crease,
curling around a thumb on a palm
cupped for rain, as nerve endings of
sea working into the land, I imagine
you as a thought, sudden then
dwindling, fat but thinning, fanning
out and light goes to ash, blurs
with words on page and a chorus
of frogs on the far bank finds voice

you lap at your name
                      a waterbird's
wings on surface out of sight break
the air into syllables and I've
remembered everything but not found
stopping as you slink by, gauze
bandage unravelling, a test tube on
its side, syringe in use spending
yourself in sea

you spill out your name

the congregation of tuarts
stands shabby while your surface
has gone to pewter and the diff-
erence is ocean has barlines of
waves and the measure of tide while
you are one endless bar played
at gravity's tempo and a chitta-
chitta flits electric and the sky?
the sky unpaints itself
                              there's a
moist fungi whiff to your name

this polyphony of drips from
leaves into bracken, you below
moving like slow animation as
stopping starts to intinct and a
raven arcs and measures the width
of silence that dwells here and
there, lights in the A-frame wink,
hint at warmth
                        and you've scabbed
and grieved for your name
                                       I've come
to you between light and none,
late afternoon luminescent and soon
rain will pucker your skin as a
clutch of small birds thumbtacks this
hessianed scape, the A-frame sitting
brighter and somewhere South fresh
gifts to brine

your name gushes from the mouth

       though your eyes are large
with moon now you are the blind river,
a reminder, creek become creed,
mantra to my stopping and A-frame
tugs at this page of none and
night clouds smirr
           you seep both sides
of your name

song of other

asleep you are lithe
curled between weed and floater,
a song of other

I stoop, hold and let
your whispers find stone, find tide,
asleep you are so lithe

then unravelling
gift of whiteness undefined,
one song of other

cadence of gather
and exhalation, waves' rush,
asleep you and lithe

turned on memory's
wheel as the spume chases day,
lost song of other

now trapped in forget,
a dust from moon's ne'er seen side,
asleep you are lithe,
a song of other

on couch

assume you die tonight,
assume they find it all,
that's a creed I can live with

chase shadows across bollards,
moon using its fine brush,
assume you die tonight

fill the box with water,
goldfish will glide 'tween bones.
that's a creed I can live with

catalyst of panic warming
belly against spine,
assume you die tonight

diagnosed manic,
need to see the back door from front.
that's a creed I can live with

on flannelette? no,
bed of freshly cut couch, but
assume you die tonight.
that's a creed I can live with

not forgottens

these six not-forgottens,
blue for a winter of reasons,
on the surface, sunlight through them

they've keened their way forward,
swum to the front of the temporals
these six not-forgottens

in the pink lake of memory,
beyond salted froth of angst, now
on the surface, sunlight through them

you left them in a train, of course,
in a tea chest, art-deco frame
these six not-forgottens

you left them, only these ripples
aren't from wind or tide,
across the surface, sunlight through them

you make a ladle with your hand,
scoop, but they evade
these six not-forgottens
on the surface, sunlight through them

Thursday's child

was born neither second nor fourth
but inbetween, fractional,
an irrational child

was born Thursday's child, far to go,
too feeble for the journey

was never drinking sky,
never lost to wonder,
just a scuffed heart,
swarm of unrhymed

was asked, half-grown,
to cease flensing.
replied 'are I?'

was the edge of language,
smirred by light

skin

you walk the land that first breathed
and flamed you. there's space, as if
God got bored, stopped, left the rest
to mind's eye. scrub lies low, in
sulk, on the scrim, hills. a hawk
loops, spins sky, drops, dives through you,
sews you back to ache and need.

you talk to clouds, sing the wind,
on your back, hours spent with weeds,
slow seep of damp. then called, home,
to dine on hush and bleed and
grief. hands froze then, on the wheel
that stole. 'you won't leave'. you don't
stay. you take the first that lands

out here

out here, a different
quality of silence, as if
sifted, as if wrung of

possibility, as
if notes, the missing fourth and sev-
enth from a pentaton-

ic scale. out here no dis-
sonance, out here where the fur of
thought won't crackle static,

out here just a pethi-
dined blue. here you let, here you pause
and permit then pour, here

you lick behind shadows, find flight,
propose theories for deja vu

just feathers

in a switched-on sky
the hawk spirals, watches, drops,
grass gifting softly

script of mimicry
as gun raises. from afar
no crack, just feathers

cupped palms

the circumference
of delusion is deduced
by multiplying

the radius of
dream with two times the height of
the pie in the sky.

the surface area of
doubt is found by tak-
ing the inverse proportion

of belief and multiply-
ing with three times the
length of the spinal column.

the volume of grief
is measured by displacement,
directing the ov-

erflow of fret and
shock from the tub of mind in-
to rows of cupped palms

a jetty all too soon

we slept like those grubs that drop from
the boughs of Tasmanian Blue Gums –

loosely tangled, squirming and writhing,
blind to our predicament, but with our

bellies thrown open to the moon for
stories to seed and flourish, for our

hunger to be sated by echoes.
we scurried and swarmed beneath you

mother, you, in the jaundiced light of
afternoons, shambolic, on spangled

summer mornings with butterflies flitting
from your mouth, a rhapsody. we grew

stunted from lack of touch, rubbed fingers
across braille of night, licked at islands

and long grass. we were soluble, bound
to the idea of loss, we were

thickets in drizzle, cropped too close and
with too dark a hue for use, we were

dry seeded. and when the leaving came
we jumped from you, a jetty all too soon

flotsam of crows

out, out into stillness
where the litter of one-shot rum bottles
keeps me mulling.
on the morrow, the moon will flesh fully,
sing as one.
like a cloak, scent of mother sits on me.
oncology – correct number of syllables,
vowelled end grinning without cadence.
I'm back walking the ward now,
not looking through doors,
walking 'neath the rain of fluorescence,
a hiss I won't hear
until I leave.
shards of imagery in rude sunlight –
wet hessian skin across the back of her hand,
taut where drip fits neat into vein,
the feeding sea.
rum bottles, 50 ml, the wrong feeding?
out in stillness, an ache through me,
like a jazz chord –
minor ninth – unresolved.
piano notes decay and through the
haze of unthinking,
intinct mood.
plastic decays, faux stained glass,
flotsam of crows.
skin frays to kin,
the hour chosen

small religion

it's as if, roaming these back streets and lanes,
you're writing a small religion, a haiku

of creeds. it's honesty, a symphony of
missing pickets and dropped fruit. the tongue

is bleeding, but the words come out the same.
checking spelling, cursive immaculate,

an orderly flight of birds across a
yellowing page. some forgottens, of course,

won't be worded. whose hours are those dressed
as cirrus? who connects the whirr of moth wings

to make theory? at these moments the hand
stutters, moves like cut-up water. and some,

some here might make a diagnosis. undiluted,
urgent, serrated thinkings. you've entered this pact

between disease, a second hand and all that's
left and in between. 'inside 18 months',

the doctor's eyes upon you. here in the lane
watching ants, the blind search for sweetness

between ten and twelve

so yes, spend a few moments
upside down. tilt on that see-saw
of nontruth and unfiction. chase

a déjà vu or two – they come
in flocks. meet no one's gaze – exchanges
in sight bring friction. do sonnet

breathing – in for eight, out for six.
you are the blind river, ever
feeling t'wards sea. gravity

is the friend, is the tempo.
you're four, spinning, spinning, giddy
in sunshine. place a tape measure

around your solitude. there's a
half-gibbous moon waiting – swim to it

the time of crows

back in the time of
crows, a childhood room, plastic
Spitfire at angle

of battle, dreams beyond fit-
ting parts and sleek black
coats, wings were everything then

venetians

thin slits of
childhood,
louvres one
breath beyond,
slicing mopoke
into up-
per, low.
it is not
raining.
thwart
the dawn,
load the
bobbin.
hour turns from
purple
to brown to
yellow.
moon
curdles night.
a week
without
seeing daylight.
illness
has
dreams overdue.
a mouth
can shape
words,
a tongue bleeds
them

the silence

we drove there in. zigzags of
sticky tape. the lump in the squashed.

we drove home. one to go with
Dad. in silence. family pet.

cardboard box. the four of us.
the squashed cardboard box. we

drove home. seemed too small.
on the back seat. Mum had said.

sticky tape too carelessly applied.
home in silence. said I should

be the one. drove home, me,
Dad. the lump too small. fifteen

years. the dog. the silence

on a Sat.

we played out dreams. we
stole flames. we boiled snails.
we strafed ants' nests. we
singed our hair. we got
called in. we got told
off. we scrubbed our nails.
we had roast. we ate
our veg. we sang and
jigged and spun. we got
tucked in. we got told
tales. we felt hot breath.
we heard our prayers. we
shared the dark. we shed
fear. we dreamt of play

Con's, 1968

on Saturday mornings, whose recurrence had an especially
unscripted and lost-kite feeling,
days linked to early or mid-autumn,
the boy went out with his father,
headed for the shops.
every time he was first taken to Ampol –
'fuel, tyres, oil, water' –
bowser man, man of nod, not word
in pressed blue short sleeves, his father,
more chatty, in white singlet, stooped over
undoing tyre air-nozzle caps

then further, to a working-class suburb where
green-grocer and hardware sat side by side.
on every occasion he had to pass houses with
hedge fences, dense green but trimmed,
resembling the work of both nature's frenzy, wilful secateurs

everything happened in such a mannered atmosphere.
in the first place, it was the leaving and
returning home on a day fat with chance,
a day that promised ever, delivered rituals –
midday closures, backyard burns.
for morning it was moving through the older 'burb,
asbestos and rendered brick homes,
buffalo or couch grass verged, spindly box trees
scratching sky. finally, it was to hear up close
the barter and banter of customer and worker
at Con's, the greengrocer's

smells and colours in that atmosphere had
so much depth, sharpened somehow and made pungent,
vivid, their tangs and hues heightened.
here were the fruit stands – peaches, plums, muscat grapes,
over which reigned the dark green roundness
of watermelon, sometimes cut open
to reveal inside its cool red and white freshness.
here were crates of vegetables – celery, brussel sprouts,
capsicum, slurred surfaces of pumpkin,
polished burnt earth of eggplant. and the shop workers
themselves, aproned, pencils behind ears, adding
prices down and around edges of newspaper,
Con, with his harelip, yelling 'cookin' grannies,
chip price!' across the display

and always, above the boy and his father, above
all the glazed fruit brilliance, ripened waft,
above scrawled crayon prices, cut-away boxes
and wheeled trolleys of shoppers, above floated
this found kinship, shoulder to shoulder, breaths
of many, uncladding of souls from the few
who, between exchange of coins and purchase,
turned, talked, let themselves of a softer blood

both ends of now

as a kid I chased infinity,
caught it between two mirrors, flesh scraped from the
back of one held, a bloodless tunnel

took it with me, to my bed-
room wardrobe, as a kid, afternoons
stoned on moment, cut on why

my shagpile mind holds this stain, scent of
wet books and radiated air, seeping through,
me still a kid, at both ends of now

also

I walk through the dimness of our childhood rooms
and I touch nothing. I walk and I'm nine and

in bed watching the model Spitfire climb then
spiral earthward. I walk and the smell of the rug

in the sleepout takes me to days of rain and
plastic soldiers, nights when louvres slivered the

mopoke's call. I walk, shifting only the furniture
of thought, and as I walk, in the folds of

Art Deco and American Bungalow and late afternoon
silence, there is plainchant, a thin vein of notes

as if someone has fused blood and music, Latin text
that sews and spells me. and these notes are father

in falsetto, these notes us, family, our Dorian joy,
major sixth intentions, flat seventh acceptance,

never medicine but a muted room, these notes are from
the fifth of us that went into that room,

stayed behind, sat still and let the loud world
pass by, then rose and left to walk into the sea

(for the siblings)

they are there on the cusp of a
little hill, in the trampled splendour

of a suburban yard. they are three,
elephantine trunks standing against a

background of untidy sky, their oily
confidences drab on Escher limbs,

and the still bricks and lost pickets
heighten the haecceity of these three.

I go and sit with them often. I sit
between them, face to a bleary just-risen

moon and while breathing deeper and deeper
I find a kind of un-stringed puppetness

owning me. everything around them is
not tinted, a landscape of slow bleeds

with aching grace: the cusp where they stand,
splashes of buffalo, pot-bellied air,

the impressionist light. some spire in a nearby
church tolls its god, and in the corduroy silence

that follows, this join-the-dots man of me
forgets numbers, this seep of leaving

rooted in turn in the clear outline of these three
draws me towards them. having no need for eyes

I follow the scent of sweet decay,
let my soles find exposed pasts, and since

no one is around, I brush my cheek
across them, hold them, press my chest

against them, know their ribbed unknowns

in the end

in the end when he went it was
so quick. in the end he was seated
in kitchen chair, as if

writing a letter, as if listening
to the wireless, as if thinking.
in the end he was in

sandals and white singlet with
slicked back white hair, mouth slightly

ajar as if beginning to speak.
in the end it was the shell
of him, the carapace,

the very empty box of him.
in the end he wasn't there,
me ready to tell him I was

the golden mean

my father, eighty years ago, at the age of –
my guess – seven – was driven

with classmates in a bus on a
stifling hot February day to a Wagin salt lake,

marched to jetty end, and thrown in.
my father never talked about the ease of floating,

how their bodies formed spoons on the surface in the
spangled light, how tepid brine burned

at lips and scabbed knees, never told us
how a girl screamed when her foot found a sheep's skull,

how three ducks watched from near the reeds, how the absence
of showers left them all with hair like dolls.

he did talk about the golden mean, ratio of weight to air,
that day, his first lesson in flight

Also available from Fremantle Press

1

FREMANTLE POETS

NEW POETS

Emma Rooksby · Scott-Patrick Mitchell · J.P. Quinton

Edited by Tracy Ryan